# Poetry of a
## Mountain Man

### By JLHubbard

ISBN-13: 978-1481858939

CopyRight ©James Lewis Hubbard June 2012

# Table of Contents

| | |
|---|---|
| INTRODUCTION | iv |
| PREFACE | v |
| Poetry of the Mountains | 6 |
| We Dare To Dream | 7 |
| That I May Fly | 8 |
| A Man's Tears | 9 |
| A Way Out | 10 |
| Passing thru | 11 |
| The Artist | 12 |
| Mood of Love | 13 |
| The Blessing | 14 |
| Paris Love | 15 |
| Manly Love | 16 |
| From Jimmy | 17 |
| What Words | 18 |
| No Words | 19 |
| Manhood | 20 |
| The Journey | 21 |
| Doubt | 22 |
| Country Serenade | 23 |
| Man Out of Control | 24 |
| A poet speaks of war | 25 |
| Love's Control | 26 |
| Night Walks | 27 |
| Good Morning Love | 28 |
| Riding Faith | 29 |
| The Choice | 30 |
| The Barrier | 31 |
| Days Gone By | 32 |
| No Traces | 33 |
| The Squirrel | 34 |
| The Light | 35 |
| Simple Pleasures | 36 |
| My Pets | 37 |
| The Sensitive Man | 38 |
| A Little Wisdom | 39 |
| Flowers on Graves | 40 |
| The Treasure | 41 |
| Faith | 42 |
| Ice man | 43 |

| | |
|---|---|
| On wisdom | 44 |
| On Sex | 45 |
| On Judging | 46 |
| Horizons | 47 |
| Obligation | 48 |
| Visions | 49 |
| Hope | 50 |
| Victims | 51 |
| Our Love | 52 |
| On Education | 53 |
| On Success | 54 |
| A Real Man | 55 |
| On cooking | 56 |
| The Flying Squirrel (Gabby Douglas) | 57 |
| The Goal | 58 |
| Tomorrow | 59 |
| The Willow Weepers | 60 |
| Mountain Man | 61 |
| Country Life | 62 |
| Florida Woman | 63 |
| Song for the Daffodil | 64 |
| Sing America | 65 |
| History Marched in Silence | 66 |
| God's Dilemma | 67 |
| A Calm Gentle Breeze | 68 |
| Granddaddy Rob | 69 |
| Homeless Humanity | 70 |
| Debt to God | 71 |
| Arrogance | 72 |
| Bond of Trust | 73 |
| These Mountains | 74 |
| Good People | 75 |
| Beauty ain't just in the Eye | 76 |
| A Better person | 77 |
| Competition and Greatness | 78 |

# INTRODUCTION

I was born and raised in the Blue Ridge Mountain which, in my opinion, was an ideal place to grow up. My father died when I was four years old, so I grew up with a void even though there were excellent role models of manhood, such as my grandfather and my uncles. So to fill that void, I found comfort in art and poetry.

"Poetry of a Mountain Man" is a collection of some of the poetry that I have been writing over a span of 30 years. Though at first glance some of the poems seem somewhat depressing, in reality they were a form of therapy, or means to work through difficult times and situations. One might say that they helped get me over my mountains. One example is the poem "From Jimmy" which helped to release some of the emotional pain of my Mother's death. It was my way of saying goodbye and letting go.

Some of the poems are observations of life. For example, "Ode to the Daffodils" is a dedication to all young people who live too fast, and die young as a result, and not my sons who are very much alive. There were times when I was very concern that they would endure the faith of the daffodil. Some of the poems are answers to questions repeated by people with apparently little interest in thinking the question though before asking it. An example of this would be "A Man's Tears".

I sincerely hope you enjoy this little book of poetry, and perhaps something in it touches you.

# PREFACE

I would like to thank all of the people who influenced me in my life. Though some are deceased, they still had quite an impact on me. My father, whom I always felt was watching. My Grandfather Rob, who though short in statute, was a giant in character and heart. My Uncle Robert and Great Uncle Clarence, who shared a pinch of their brilliance. I would like to think my brothers and sisters for accepting me the way I am...strange. I would also like to thank my children; Krystal, Marcellus, and Jamel for we kinda had to grow up together.

More importantly, I would like to thank the two people in whose love gave me strength and kept me somewhat straight. I would like to thank my Mother, and best friend, Geneva (deceased), and my wife, and best friend, Deborah. I often wish that they could have met. Deborah, I love you.

Most importantly, I would like to thank God for giving me the tools and talent to help me see over the mountains.

## Poetry of the Mountains

I see the poetry of the mountains
Majestic in their stand
Whether they have lush greenery,
Or merely sun baked sand.

I see the skyline of the cities,
And their thousands of glittering lights.
imitating stars sparkling,
On a beautiful cloudless night.

I hear the roar of the ocean's waves
Serenading the sandy shores
The gentle breeze enhances their song
And the palm trees cry encore.

Yes, I read the poetry of all these wonders
Like a book that never end.
Enjoying the beauty that they offer,
brings me peace within.

# We Dare To Dream
*(Written in honor of Gen. Colin Powell)*

    What meager reward shall be redeemed
    to those of us who dare to dream.

    We ignore the boundaries of where we are,
    and gaze upon an unseen star.
    Extending our limits until we fall in vain,
    only to rise and do it over again.

    If you find our graves along life's path
    carved in stone will be this epitaph
    "We may not have reached all of our goals
    it seems, but we would not be this far.....
                    Had we not dare to dream."

## That I May Fly

My life was spent gazing at the sky,
silently wishing that I could fly.
How ridiculous a wish it seemed
that a grown man should have such a dream.
Then came one glorious day
when I shed my doubt and flew away.

## A Man's Tears

I have cried for a million nights
and for a million nights tears fell like rain.
But no one has heard my gentle sighs,
and by day the shadows hide my pain.

Deeply into my pillow I cling
and muffle the sounds of my own soft weeping.
For no one would think to cuddle this man,
and comfort me as I lay sleeping.

I must be careful not to give away
a secret that all men must carry.
Inside each man there is a child,
in stone emotion we're forced to bury.

It is not our choosing, but what is taught
for it is often said that real men don't cry.
So we continue to cry for a million nights,
while deep in our pain-soaked beds we lie.

## A Way Out

One day
I'll drift away.
  One day
  I know.
      One day
      It won't matter.
        One day
        I'll just go.
          One day
          I'll disappear.
            One day
            I won't come back
            One day
            I just won't care
            One day
            I'll fade to black.
            One day
            I'll drift away.

## Passing thru

We're only here for a little while,
to shed a tear and exchange a smile.
For life is a brief lonely aisle,
that we are only passing thru.

We're put here simply to run the race.
Whether we follow or set the pace,
no one wins a permanent place,
cause we are only passing thru.

We're given this brief life to bare,
and search to find some reason to care.
For these moments are sweeter
if we can share,
                    as we are passing thru.

## The Artist

    Oh tis with great pain we try
    to extend ourselves and touch the sky.

    Those looking on... often ridicule
    this daring attempt executed by a fool.

    The artist has simply one curse
    within our mortal minds...
        we hold the universe.

## Mood of Love

Let us go back to a simpler time,
and drink the nectar of a primitive wine.
Listen to the sounds of our heart beat,
and dance to that rhythm so savage and sweet.

Let us lay naked in each other's embrace,
and permit raw passion to set its own pace.
Our song will be song without an end,
as we find the true mood of love again.

## The Blessing

I said a prayer late one night
different from the prayers before.
I said, "Lord send me someone to love."
I didn't ask for anything more.

I didn't give any specifications,
no education, height or weight.
I said, "Lord just send me a good woman,
and you can't find one right away-I'll wait."

Now the Lord really knows me well
he was with me since my life begun.
So the only thing I tacked on to the prayer
was "whatever thou will be done".

Now things don't always happen right away
as a matter of fact it took a while.
But one day when I was attending church,
I saw this pretty woman smile.

Truly a blessing I must say,
cause this woman I've grown to adore.
Not only did the Lord send me what I needed.
But Praise God , he send me so much more.

## Paris Love

I never really believed in love at first sight
until I went to Paris one night
I don't mean to mislead you.... see
I fell in love with the whole city.

So much culture in one little place,
 and so much character on every passing face
As I looked about it seemed
to be a writer's paradise and an artist's dream.

Now I could bore you out of your head,
but it won't matter what I've said.
So I'll leave with these little lines like this
and share a touch of the joy,
      that I got from Paris

## Manly Love

Tell them now, that you love them,
and thank them for the love they gave.
It does no good to wait in silence,
and utter it on a cold dark grave.

It is not manly to live in silence,
and keep emotions concealed;
but foolish to have a heart of love
without expressing how you feel.

Many Men have traveled thru life
with feelings they're afraid to show.
They loose people they deeply love
without ever letting them know.

If there is one lesson that I've learned
Through out my many years,
it is the brave men that show their love,
and the strong ones will even show tears.

# From Jimmy

Mama,
If I could have found the words to say,
all that you've done before you passed away.
I wanted you to know before you were gone,
that on the wings of you love, I would sail on.

And Mama,
If only I could have had a little more time,
to sit on your bed and read you this rhyme.
You taught me to love and treat people right,
and never give up without a good fight.

But Mama,
I must go now and let you rest,
for you have run your race and done your best.
I wish for a small portion of your success.
Farewell, my best friend, and may God Bless.

## What Words

What do you say to a person dying,
that comfort him and ease his fears?
What can you do for a baby crying,
but only to embrace it and wipe its tears?

But sadder yet is a person laying,
hopelessly in life it seems.
There are no words or clever sayings,
for those who lost the will to dream.

## No Words

How do I say
that the time has come
for us to love?

What words do I use
to persuade you
to trust in our love?

No words can erase
the pain you felt
from other loves.

How cruel of life
to put such love in my heart...
and no word to my lips.

# Manhood

You cannot reach manhood, my son,
and continue to be a brat.
For though the mind is very complex,
the head can only wear one hat.

# The Journey

Inch by inch to mile by mile
is the way I travel this road.
Ounce by ounce to ton by ton
weighs the burden of my load.

Hurt by hurt to tear by tear
measures the depth of my grief.
Second by second to year by year
still the time seems far too brief.

Love by love to friend by friend
are the treasures I find along the way.
Joy by joy to pleasure by pleasure
keeps me going another day.

Smile by smile to laughter by laughter
are fruits I pick along the trail,
and dream by dream to goal by goal
are the winds - that sets my sail.

## Doubt

Is this true love I see in your eyes?
Do my own eyes dare to believe?
To experience the joy of love returned,
or the pain of a heart again deceived.

Is this real love I feel in your touch?
Do love and lust feel the same?
Do moments and eternity share the same space?
Or reality and falsehood harbor the same pain?

If the love and lust of your eyes and touch
bring only deceit and pain for me.
Then it is better to embrace a moment of eternity,
and remember it with love - as it should be.

## Country Serenade

While Lying in bed
trying to sleep,
I heard the lullaby
of a cricket's weep.

The frog rejoicing
his croaking has filled
the background music
of the whip-o-will.

The soft love songs
of the meadow lark
in harmony with the creek
rushing over rocks.

I wonder if there
is anyone but me
who enjoys being serenaded
by this country symphony.

## Man Out of Control

One day,
I will reach to the stars,
and select the ones I want,
and pluck the rest from the sky.

And then,
I will harness the wind,
and travel the continent
as I please.

And then,
I will discover the secret of love,
and use it on whomever I please
as I please.

But then
the only thing
left uncontrolled
will be my selfish greed.

## A poet speaks of war

There is nothing more that I deplore
than nations choosing to go to war
Men killing men, bombs killing kids
It's like our soul is in the gamble,
but we don't realize the bid.

## Love's Control

Once my love ran free
like a raging stream,
it was too beautiful for reality,
yet, too clear for a dream.

Its currents were strong,
and its course was true.
It washed away the ghosts
of the pain I knew.

So electrifying was its force,
so deep and wide,
that my lover tried to control it.
It grew stale and died.

# Night Walks

My lovely lady who walks with me.
a warm silent shadow of serenity.
I am part of you, and you of me,
for our hearts have vowed this to be.

Oh lady, my lady, I must confess
in these brief moments I truly feel blessed.
Though my life was once filled with loneliness,
you touched my hand and our hearts did the rest.

Come, my lady, our hearts must soar
beyond all hardships we had to endure.
If in our journey we must face more,
remember, our love is the key to heaven's door.

## Good Morning Love

Awaken my love, the day has begun.
Open your eyes to the morning sun.
Last night's dreams can surely be won,
for love came in with the dawn.

Let love not pass us in our sleeping,
or clinging to yesterday's weeping.
Today is ours for the keeping,
for love crept in with the dawn.

Let love not find us with emotions hidden,
or passions harnessed, and not freely ridden.
No pleasures in life will be forbidden,
when love rides in with the dawn.

This morning has come for us to face
in the warm sun's rays, we shall embrace,
and here on this day, we will find our place,
and let our love grow bright with the dawn.

## Riding Faith

Faith, is like a beautiful racehorse
it cannot perform well...
when you dig your knees into its side,
or, pull back it's reigns in fear.

But Faith is at its best
when you relax....
loosen the reigns...
trust in its power.

And Faith....
will bring you home
every time.

## The Choice

I do not believe the path of a lifetime
should be taken with a moment's thought,
for my closet is full of broken dreams,
and bad judgments hastily bought.

I do not feel a debt should be made
without the interest and penalty weighed,
for my life is full of careless ventures,
and haunting ghosts of debts unpaid.

But it does not matter right or wrong,
for there are few foresights to our mistakes,
the responsibility is ours to carry the blame,
and pay the dues for the choices we make.

# The Barrier

We build these barriers
so safe and warm
to protect ourselves
from other's harm.

So deep these barriers
that we hide in,
that we doubt our lovers,
and mistrust our friends.

So strong this fortress,
that we built so well,
what was meant to protect us
has become our jail.

## Days Gone By

I have learned not to sit and cry
over pass events of days gone by.
There is no need to retrace my tracks,
and the past is too heavy for my back.

I have spent my life it seems
reaching for rainbows and chasing dreams,
but the dreams that are lost without a try
are the saddest memories of days gone by.

## No Traces

Remember those cold wintry days
when we were filled with love and desire.
We warmed each other from the cold
with the heat from our passion's fire.

But now your footprints in the snow
are the only traces that linger on,
and there will come a bright sunny day
when they too will be gone.

# The Squirrel

A squirrel came to visit on this autumn day
in search of food to store away.
It banged its head on my windowpane,
and relentlessly tried again and again.

Surely this creature must be insane
to make such an attempt in spite of the pain.
Perhaps, it believes that the glass will fall,
or mere determination can conquer all.

Should I reward its foolish deeds
with a meager bounty of a hand full of seeds?
But reward it I did, for in its brief strife,
I saw reflections - reflections of my own life.

# The Light

I often feel so out of place,
and out of touch with reality.
This world a so-called rat-race,
seems all merely a show to me.

I see the sadness in this cruel world,
full of hurt, dishonesty and pain,
and refrain myself from retaliation,
for it reaps no reward or gain.

I embed myself in my own dreams
and live what I believe is right,
For in this cold world of darkness,
Truth shall be my heat and light.

## Simple Pleasures

I remember the simpler times,
as intoxicating as vintage wines.
I sat under those large shade trees,
and felt the passing of a soft gentle breeze.

I would lay for hours staring at the sky
imagining figures in the cloud passing by.
Beside me the sparkling brook would creep,
its sound gently put me to sleep.

I lingered in the moments of those lazy days,
and somehow, they don't seem wasted away.
Though life we often gain many treasures,
and some are the memories of simple pleasures.

## My Pets

I once had three ugly dogs, you know.
They would follow me wherever I go.
Those were not happy moments for me,
so, I named them Trouble, Pain, and Misery.

It seems as if they were always at my side,
and always found me if I tried to hide.
Well... they're gone now, but there's no relief,
they left me a puppy....I named him Grief.

## The Sensitive Man

Many women that I meet today
want to explore my sensitive side,
and some will even go out of their way
to find the scars and wounds I hide.

It's not that I'm afraid of losing control,
or have trouble expressing how I feel,
but I must question their hidden goal,
and if their concerns are sincere and real.

Is it that they really care for me,
and want to be there for all my needs,
or might it be mere curiosity
to reopen my wounds and leave me to bleed?

## A Little Wisdom

A little dining and a lot of wine,
that woman sure did treat me fine.
A little partying and a lot of beer,
and she told me things I wanted to hear.

But a little hard-time and a lot of poor,
and she said she wasn't my woman no more.
A little struggling and a lot of pain,
and I got myself together again.

A little begging and a lot of pleading,
and she says it's me she's really needing.
A little wisdom and a lot of cool,
and I told her to find another fool.

## Flowers on Graves

Are the flowers placed on loved one's graves
a plea for our own souls to be saved?
It's not that they can smell them laying there,
but more a need to still show we care.

No summer sun nor winter snow
can disturb these people's final sleep.
Yet we stand there and let tears flow
renewing the promises we vowed to keep.

But in these brief moments of sorrow and tears,
and painful reflections of previous years.
We take these moments with comforting breaths
and know that love is even stronger than death.

## The Treasure

Come, my lady, let us not fight
for my struggle is not with you.
I do not seek to control the night,
but gain trust in the things I do.

we must set forth together
in heart and mind.
and struggles we meet
strengthen the ties that bind.

We will make dreams reality
and seize the secret of life's pearl.
That the real treasure will always be
you and I standing against the world.

## Faith

We continue to travel these rugged roads
though burdens weigh us down.
The relief we seek from our load
seldom seems to be found.

We never fully understand,
but always try to find,
some divine creator's plan
to provide us with peace of mind.

It is by faith we carry the weight
and the creator's plan is divine.
For there is a purpose to every faith,
and to every faith a time.

# Ice man

*Once I was...*
　　someone warm
　　someone caring
　　someone honest
　　someone friendly.

　　*But the world was...*
　　　　something cold
　　　　something indifferent
　　　　something dishonest
　　　　something unfriendly.

*So I became...*
　　someone cold
　　someone uncaring
　　someone deceitful
　　someone bitter

　　*But I became...*
　　　　someone...
　　　　*I did not like.*

## On wisdom

A person never gains true wisdom
until he overcomes the fear
of appearing foolish.
The old wise ones today
were yesterday's young fools.

## On Sex

Sex is like a piece of cake.

Sex with love...
it is an eloquent desert
after a fine meal.

Sex without love...
it is merely a snack.

## On Judging

People ask me what I think
about pro-choice
and gay marriage.
I say..............
It's none of my business

God gave me many talents, but..
he never gave me
the right to judge others.
he reserves that right
and I'm not going to
try to do his job.

## Horizons

When you reach your horizon,
will there be a place for me?
Will we at last find our precious sun,
or the cold shadows of a memory?

If we never find our moment,
and all magic of moments are gone.
Remember me as you left me standing,
loving and hurting - but cheering you on.

## Obligation

I feel a sense of obligation
for those who gave me a chance
Whether it was employment,
or mere just a dance.

There are many I meet in life
who think they made it on their own
but no makes it without someone's help,
or dances through life alone.

# Visions

I see visions of things to come...
two people bathing in love's warm rays.
Where one plus one will find the sum
of lovers embracing loneliness away.

I see the pain of future and past
of halves trying to become a whole.
As long as the moments last
tis bittersweet the bonding of their souls.

Yes, I see visions of things to come...
and feel that faith will beckon me.
Afraid the moment will never come,
and praying that it is still to be.

Oh sweet vision, cradle my fright.
I shall not fall, but still hold tight.
It is in that vision that my heart takes flight,
and forgets it sleep alone again tonight.

# Hope

Where are the dreams that go unanswered,
or cries of the lost when no one responds?
Do they fall like rain into mighty streams,
or scream like the wind across the ponds?

When life passes from hope to hopeless,
is there no point of time or space?
Are there no footsteps along that border,
for those seeking desperately to retrace?

Cast you dreams upon those waters,
and scream your cries into the wind.
It is thru these acts of desperation,
that we find the path to hope again.

# Victims

We are all victims of ourselves,
prisoners of some insecurity.
We all search for something else
to break our chains and set us free.

We all want to sing our song aloud,
and desperately want someone to listen.
Yet, we stand silent among the crowd,
and only the message in our eyes glistens.

We all walk about as if being haunted
by the burden of the price of living.
Small is weigh of not being wanted,
to that of the love we are afraid of giving.

We cannot rely on gestures or words
to break our dams so love can pour.
For love is like a mighty bird,
and only we can free it and let it soar.

## Our Love

Lying in bed watching you sleep,
I thought of our love and began to weep.
These were not tears of pain or distress,
but a heart overflowing with happiness.

Just the thought that after all these years,
after all the pain and all the tears.
I would be so bless to find
a love that gave me true peace of mind.

I began to tremble and lose my nerve,
feeling that my blessing is more than I deserve.
I leaned over and kissed you as you slept
and made a vow that I have always kept.

To love you deeply with all of my heart,
and always cherish you as a gift from God.
My life is full now and know little strife
for God blessed me with a best friend
    who is my wife.

## On Education

People stress to their kids
get a good education
so you can get
a good job.

A good education does not
guarantee a good job.
and the basis for learning
should not be employment.

The basis for learning
should be achieving knowledge,
and formal education is not
the only place to obtain it.

I didn't enjoy learning
until I had finished school
and now, over thirty years later
I still enjoy learning

I may not have had the best jobs
but the knowledge that I have gained
in learning from books and life
is priceless.

## On Success

People often have long
complicated criteria
for defining success

In reality there is only one
It's not money
nor fame, or friends

The definition of success...
is happiness

I've heard of rich,
and famous, and popular people
ending their lives

I have never heard
of someone committing suicide
because they were just too damn happy.

## A Real Man

When I was a child
I wanted to be a strong man
so I imitated
what strong men did

When I was a young man
I wanted to be a good man
so I imitated
what good men did

As I grew older
I wanted to be a real Man
so I imitated
what I thought real men did

When I finally matured
I decided to be my own man
that was the moment
that I became all three.

## On cooking

I remember, as a young boy,
watching my mother cook
It was the few times
we had a chance to talk.

When I grew up,
I discovered
that I enjoyed cooking
like I enjoyed art.

One time my mother came for a visit
and I prepared dinner
My mother said
"Boy, this good where did you learn to cook?"

I smiled and said I learned by watching you
Plus I added a little something
I could see pride in her eyes
as we finished our meal.

My mother has been gone
for over twenty years,
but sometimes when I cook..
I can still feel her spirit...
                       and that pride.

# The Flying Squirrel (Gabby Douglas)

I watched her on the uneven bars
dotting back and forth
like a squirrel in trees
Is this how she got her name?

During her acrobatic routine
people waited for her to fall
like dogs watching a squirrel
Perhaps this is how she got her name

She did not fall or fumble
but soared with such ease and grace
Ah, maybe this is
how she got her name

When the time came for her dismount
she soared high above the bars with spectacular flips
and returned to the earth landing on her feet
Oh, I bet this is how she got her name

As I recalled Gabby's routine
I realized that this was symbolic of her life
She will always be on the uneven bars of life
and she will always be soaring high above those bars
        and this is how she will earn her name

## The Goal

I have always had one goal
to have one lover to watch me grow old.
To find that mate to be my best friend,
and grow so close, she'll look like my twin.

To be so close to someone, you see,
that if I have a thought, she'll finish it for me.
I've seen some couples, or so it seems,
so I know my quest is a reachable dream.

Though the years may bring loneliness,
I hold on to my goal and accept nothing less.

## Tomorrow

How many people in these little grave hills
had charged their life on tomorrow's bills.
Only to die without their dreams fulfilled
for they were not promised tomorrow.

How many living have chosen to wait.
They meditate, contemplate, and procrastinate,
if they're dreams don't come true - they blame faith
cause they were not promised tomorrow.

We must set forth for our place in the sun
for yesterday is dead and tomorrow's undone.
Today is the only day dreams can be won
for we are not promised tomorrow.

# The Willow Weepers

We went to the pond, my love and I,
down where the willows sway
to the gentle breezes passing by.
Beneath the tree we spent the day.

We made our promises, my love and I,
to love even beyond this life.
The breeze carried the vows across the sky
as I carved that tree with my knife.

I go to the pond, alone am I,
the promises are just memories.
The breeze is silent - not a sigh
only the weeping of that tree and me.

# Mountain Man

I'm a mountain man, Baby,
that's what I am.
So don't give me jelly,
when I ask you for jam.

I ran barefoot in the mountains,
and swam naked in the creeks.
So just because I'm good to you,
don't try a play me weak.

I don't care about money,
or how rich you wanna live.
If I can't get simple love from you,
you ain't got nothing to give.

All I want is a good woman,
that I know will be around
to sit on the porch together,
and watch the sun go down.

Maybe in the beauty of the evening,
she'll grow to understand.
Why these things that are important
in the life of this mountain man.

## Country Life

Now I'm a old country man
with old country ways.
I like to kinda sit back a little
at the end of those country days.

I married me a country woman,
who cooks good country food.
Ain't nothing like country loving
once she gets in the mood.

Sometimes at the end of a country day,
we sat on the porch and talk
or sometimes go down the road a piece.
In city talk, that's called taking a walk.

Now I know my life may sound boring,
and you wonder how I live like this.
I guess some folk's idea of living in hell
is another's of living in bliss.

## Florida Woman

My woman is a Florida woman,
and I'm a Virginia mountain man.
I like those high mountain views,
but she likes the sun, beach, and sand.

I say "Baby, look at those roving hills.
and trees as far as the eye can see."
She looks at me unimpressed,
and say "A tree is just a tree."

She say "Look at that pretty blue water
washing on the golden shore,
and there's no lovelier sound on earth
than listening to the ocean's roar."

Well... I guess we'll live by the ocean,
and visit the mountains once in a while.
Cause the most beautiful sight to me
is still that Florida woman's smile.

## Song for the Daffodil

I sing this song for the Daffodils,
and the sweet pleasures they bring.
These golden trumpets cover the hills,
and announce the beginning of spring.

Their song is both sweet and bright,
but short-lived is their glory.
That they never live to see a summer night
is the sadness of their story.

They seem so lovely in their joyful dance,
as the March winds make them sway.
It is so tragic that this romance
is gone by the end of May.

So moved by their presentations,
and the brief living that they've done,
that with compassion and in representation,
I planted them on the grave of my son.

## Sing America

I come not to sing of injustices dealt,
nor open the wounds of suffering felt,
but in this melting pot - I come to melt.
Yes, I come to sing America.

I shall not dwell on gender or race,
but rather seek my rightful place,
and seize the dream we all embrace.
The dream of singing America.

I sing loud and sing with pride,
and welcome any at my side,
for we all have loved ones who died.
So that we can sing America.

So on this day I take my stand,
and let my tears fall upon this land,
and reach out to all with a open hand.
Who will join me in singing America.

Let America be home for me.
Let our sing be sung with such beauty,
that the eagle will at last be free.
When we all stand to sing America.

## History Marched in Silence

History marched in silence
as the lady took command.
No great fan fare,
or reporters there,
still faith dealt its hand,
and history marched in silence.

All eyes were upon her,
as she prepared to troop-the-line.
Her pace was not humble,
nor did she stumble,
but marched in perfect time.
Like history marching in silence.

Her's will be two battles
as she prepares her troops to fight.
Doubting eyes
will scrutinize
and shall surely test her might.
But history will march in silence.

The lady stood straight with pride.
her posture was not bowed.
No note was made
to the dues she paid
to get where she is now.
Still history marched in silence.

The lady is destined to make it
and surely she will know success.
The strength is there
for the burden she'll bare,
to rise among the best.
Then march on in silence.

(in honor of LTC Deborah Hollis, my wife)

## God's Dilemma

I was wondering one day
why God had chosen
 to take my mother away.

The more I wondered,
the more I got mad,
Seems he takes all the good ones
and leave all the bad.

But then I thought
what else could he do.
There's probably a shortage
of good people in heaven too.

## A Calm Gentle Breeze

I remember being a little child
with a calmness so soft and mild.
A soothing feeling that made my soul at ease
like a spring night and a calm gentle breeze.

As I grew older and saw my fellow man
stand and proclaim, "God gave me this land!"
I watched him destroy this land in civilization's name,
and marked God as though it were a game.

I saw man kill and call it a way of life,
and take the meaning of love and turn it to strife.
This child's heart that was so peaceful and warm
grew from a gentle breeze to a cold raging storm.

No matter how great the storm, it can't erase dirt,
when the roots are strong caused by years of hurt.
So if you see a man on a hill, down on his knees,
there you'll see this little child,
                    searching for his gentle breeze.

*(written at age 15)*

# Granddaddy Rob

My Grandfather was
a small man.
He stood 5'2" and 134lbs
I remember at age 15
I was 5'6" able to stand beside him
and look down at him.

Now my granddaddy was
the kindest man
He took time with us
after my father died.
He took us fishing when
He really didn't know how to fish.

And my Grandfather was
The cleanest man
I ever met…always a gentleman
His dress was impeccable,
He always smelled of soap
And aftershave or cologne

My Granddaddy was
The kind of man
That I grew to admire
And in my maturity
I find that I will always
look up to him

## Homeless Humanity

I was approached by a homeless man,
While talking on the phone one day
He said "Look man, can you spare a dollar?"
But I motion for him to go away.

After my call, I looked about
To see if he was still there
To my disappointment, it almost seemed
That he just disappeared in thin air.

I started thinking how arrogant I am
To forget when my own life was hard
We sometimes forget we need someone
some of us don't remember needing God

Next time the occasion presents itself
To show one a little charity
I will act at once before it disappears
And with it, my humanity

## Debt to God

    I have a debt to pay to God......
                I have a debt to pay.

I have been ignoring my talents
          and wasting my time

    Ignoring his will and
              selfishly following mine

But still there is the debt.

God has given us talents
           That we do not use

We whine endlessly about
           the life we choose

Still there is that debt.

When I stand before God
           I hope to have no regrets

This book is a down payments
           on those debts.

Other payments to follow...........
           cause I don't want to leave

Without his visions for me achieved

## Arrogance

I never accepted the theory
that people are better or smarter
simply because of their skin color
or their status in life

I have never smiled
when I wasn't happy,
nor been humbled
when I knew I was right.

I have spoken out
when others remained silent
I do not go along
simply to get along.

When some people behave this way
they call it virturous
but when I do it
they call it arrogance

and I never let
what they think bother me
because what matters more
is what I think of myself

## Bond of Trust

Trust creates a
bond between people
that is stronger
than most loves

Trust should be
the foundation of love
for love without trust
has little chance for survival.

Yet, some people
miss the opportunity
to be trustworthy
or trust others

It is sad when
trust is breached
because once lost
you never completely...
        get it back

## These Mountains

I was born in these mountains
these mountains are a part of me
Whenever I face life's problems
they bring me serenity

I just take my troubles to these mountains
and cast them into the sky
they fall back to earth like grains of dust
cause we all know problems can't fly

I look down into the valley
the people look so small below
I know they all have their burdens
but they don't know where to go.

Yes I was born in these mountains
though it may not be where I end
but I am not concerned
be I buried or burned
Cause my soul will find its way home again

*(from back cover)*

# Good People

Women say there are no good men left
I tell them my wife found one
Men say there are no good women left
I tell them that I found one

Good people are like gold
if they were laying on the ground
they wouldn't be valuable
you gotta dig thru some rocks

Some people don't realize the burden
that once they find a good person
they have to step up their game
and become a good person too

I have seen a lot of men and women
lose good people because
they didn't treat them like
the precious gold that they are.

So the next time you go looking
for a good man or woman
take a moment to check yourself
are YOU ready?

## Beauty ain't just in the Eye

Beauty ain't just in the eye
cause you can marry a beautiful person
with a ugly personality and soon
you'll hate the sight of them

Or you can marry a ugly person
with a beautiful personality and as time passes
they will grow more beautiful to you
Cause Beauty ain't just in the eye...

It's also in the heart.

## A Better person

Finding fault in others
and pointing out
corrective measures doesn't
make you a better person

Finding fault in yourself
and taking corrective measures
to improve yourself will
make you a better person.

Blaming others
for your life
and living in the past
won't make you a better person.

Taking responsibility
for your mistakes in life
and changing your present and future
will make you a better person.

The road to a better person
is sometimes lonely and hard
Just remember that only you
can make you a better person.

## Competition and Greatness

Never compete against
another person  in life
cause once you beat that person
you may stop growing

Instead compete against
yourself in everything in life
your potential will be endless
and you will never stop growing

Made in the USA
Charleston, SC
01 February 2013